Memories of **WOLSINGHAM**

COUNTY DURHAM BOOKS

The compilers of this book have endeavoured to contact and seek permission from the copyright holders of all the photographs used herein. If we have inadvertently used a picture without permission we would be grateful if the copyright holder would contact us so that we can make the proper acknowledgement in any future editions.

Front cover: Wolsingham Old Town Hall

© County Durham Books, 2005

All rights reserved. No part of this publication may be reproduced, stored in a retrieval system, or transmitted in any form or by any means, electronic, mechanical, photocopying or otherwise, without the prior permission of the publisher.

Published by County Durham Books, 2005

County Durham Books is the imprint of Durham County Council

ISBN 1897585845

Memories of WOLSINGHAM

I moved to Holbeck Mill from further up the dale in the spring of 1948. The Mill was situated to the west of Wolsingham, on a narrow piece of land, between the south bank of the River Wear and the railway.

It was a small self contained farm of approximately 25 acres including some scrub grazing and woodland. I was immediately captivated by the prolific and diverse nature of the flora and fauna and of Wolsingham itself, a condition which has remained with me to the present day.

The five storied corn mill, probably the last to be built on the river, was both sound and weatherproof and had a roof of blue slate and interior timbers of pitch pine. It had two sets of French mill stones, but alas, the waterwheel itself was missing.

In the photograph overleaf only a little of the corn mill can be seen to the left of the house. Towards the end of 1955 the entire mill, its adjoining three story house, up and down cottage and full range of buildings were demolished, to such an extent that it is very difficult for me to remember their original positions.

The only landmark remaining is the brick-built well, next to the railway boundary wall under two or three larch trees and covered by a large flat rock. It won't be long before anyone can remember Holbeck Mill or pass on any information about it. The only record left will be a photographic one.

Photographic records are essential in maintaining continuity of Wolsingham's history. The really old photographs of Wolsingham, taken from a time as far back as that of photography itself, are so very important to us today.

What a great loss it would have been if enthusiastic and dedicated people had not taken and preserved their photographs for the future enjoyment of anyone, like yourself, about to embark on this pictorial book Memories of Wolsingham

J.J. Anderson.

(Compiled by Wolsingham library and the people of Wolsingham)

HOLBECK MILL

Council School cricket team 1948 season.

Melbourne Place, Wolsingham.

Uppertown Wolsingham.

Mr. J.J. Aubin's outing for the wounded of the First World War. Note there are no RAF men, only Army and Navy. This photograph is taken outside the National School, now the Parish Hall (recently converted to housing).

Old Town Hall after the erection of the Monument. Note the volume of traffic and the cobbled market place! The butcher's shop at the far right of the photo is Hamiltons.

Wolsingham Working Men's Club - Members pictured in 1935 outside the club which was in Angate Street.

The Bay Horse Hotel on fire in the early 1920's.

Parish Church, Wolsingham.

Farm at Westfield, once part of the Fenwick estate.

Teachers from the Council School 1948-49.

Holywood Sanatorium, Pavillion 1.

Uppertown Wolsingham. The dog is looking towards the St. Anne's Convent. The building with the bike in front of it is the butcher's department of the Wolsingham branch of the Tow Law and District Co-operative Society.

George Shuttleworth in his car with 2 children.

The Bluestars Football team who played on a pitch at the old saw mill lonnen.

View of the sanatorium from the Tunstall Road.

Wolsingham Male Voice choir. The chairman was Mr. Downey (at the extreme right of photo). The photo was taken in the grounds of his house - Mayfield House.

Wolsingham Station. A group of people on the way to a football match.

Craig Terrace, Wolsingham. At the far left of photo you'll see the gas house chimney.

The old picture house - closed in 1963. The projector was housed in the brick building to the left of the main building.

Members of the Womens Institute arriving at the Town Hall. The lady front centre is Mrs. Meg Garraway.

Wolsingham cricket team

Wolsingham Working Mens Club in the 1920's.

Wolsingham cricket team. They were champions of the South West Durham League in 1928.

A dancing group at Wolsingham Council School (now the Primary School).

Wolsingham School children.

A street party celebrating the end of World War 2 in Melbourne Place.

Wolsingham Council School, with teacher Miss Harriet Watson on the far right.

Wolsingham Grammar School gymnasium. Note the gym uniform!

The Wolsingham Steel Works choir, taken after the World War 2, was formerly known as Wolsingham Male Voice choir.

29

The re-opening of Wolsingham market after World War 1, with the Golden Lion pub in the background (Union Jack flying). The Queens Head pub is to the far right of the photo.

The Bay Horse hotel after it was rebuilt following the fire.

Wolsingham Working Mens Club outing.

Wolsingham Home Guard 1939-45

Wolsingham cricket team.

Wolsingham Steel Works stand at Wolsingham Show.

Staff from Wolsingham Steel Works. Left to right, Stephen Parmley, Walter Boon and Tom Ridley (Personnel Manager).

Wolsingham Steel workers on the occasion of their retirement. Left to right, Matty Scorer, George Amos, John Gill and Oliver Hesp.

Wolsingham Steel Works staff from the fabrication department.

Wolsingham Steel Works staff. George Amos pictured with Billy Moore, head of the electrical department.

A view over the station bridge.

The anchor for RMS Mauritania made at the steel works.

A view of Jack Walker bridge and Holywood Hall before the sanatorium was built.

The Steel Works children's Christmas party.

The Steel Works staff.

The Sanatorium pavilion.

Holywood Hall from the garden, before the sanatorium was built.

Holywood Hall. We think this is a picture of the domestic staff.

Whitfield House in the snow.

St. Mary's Convent which later became St. Anne's Convent.

Cottages next to Whitfield House, one of the oldest houses in Wolsingham. It was formerly The Pack Horse Inn.

Walking the geese to market along Front Street.

The Old Forge along the causeway.

View of Wolsingham from Wears bank. The sanatorium is on the hillside above the church.

The bridge over Thornhope Beck at Leazes Lane.

The huts at Holywood Sanatorium.

The white painted building behind the group of men is the former Grey Bull public house. It was later demolished and rebuilt at a distance back from the road and is now the Mill Race Inn.